Contents

1 Introduction: A Global Perspective

Understanding crime necessitates a global perspective. Defining "criminality" itself proves a complex task, varying significantly across cultures. What constitutes a crime in one society might be acceptable behavior in another, highlighting the deeply subjective nature of legal definitions. Consider, for instance, the varying cultural attitudes towards drug use—some societies criminalize even minor possession, while others adopt far more lenient approaches, emphasizing harm reduction over strict prohibition. This fundamental difference underscores the need for careful contextualization when comparing crime statistics and legal frameworks internationally. A universal definition simply doesn't exist; our understanding must evolve to account for this undeniable truth. Failing to acknowledge these cultural differences risks misinterpreting data and creating flawed policy based on misguided assumptions about what constitutes 'criminal' behaviour across different societies.

The very concept of justice, too, differs drastically worldwide. Western justice systems, for example, often emphasize retribution and punishment, seeking to deter future crime through incarceration and fines. In contrast, many non-Western cultures prioritize restorative justice, focusing on reconciliation and rehabilitation rather than solely punishment. These systems often involve community-led mediation and emphasize repairing the harm caused by a crime, both to the victim and the broader community. This approach, deeply rooted in communal values, prioritizes healing and reintegration over simple punishment. The effectiveness of each approach, however, remains a matter of ongoing debate, as the ideal model often depends on specific cultural contexts and the nature of the crime committed. A holistic understanding requires acknowledging the diverse goals and methods employed in achieving 'justice'.

Furthermore, historical context profoundly shapes legal systems. Colonial legacies, for example, have left indelible marks on the legal frameworks of many former colonies, creating complex hybrid systems that blend indigenous traditions with imposed Western models. The lingering influence of colonial rule can be seen in the persistence of certain legal structures and procedures, often at odds with existing cultural values. This historical baggage presents immense challenges for contemporary legal reform efforts, as attempts to modernize legal systems must often navigate the complexities of reconciling tradition with the demands of a globalized world. A thorough investigation of these historical roots is crucial for comprehending the contemporary landscape of global crime and justice.

Comparative analysis, therefore, becomes indispensable for gaining a nuanced understanding of crime and justice globally. This requires moving beyond simple comparisons of crime rates or incarceration statistics—often unreliable and contextually deficient—and focusing instead on the underlying cultural values, historical factors, and institutional structures that shape legal responses to criminal behavior. Researchers must strive for deeper understanding of the contextual aspects of each society, avoiding broad generalizations and recognizing the multifaceted nature of cultural influences. The emphasis should be on the underlying philosophies and values that inform these diverse approaches. By understanding these nuances, we can progress toward crafting more effective and equitable justice systems.

In conclusion, this global perspective on crime is not merely an academic exercise. It is crucial for the development of effective crime prevention strategies, international collaborations on justice reform, and the promotion of human rights worldwide. This chapter has sought to provide the foundation for this deeper understanding by highlighting the cultural relativity of crime definitions and illustrating the vast diversity of justice systems across the globe. This sets the stage for a more detailed exploration of specific regional approaches throughout the remainder of this book. The challenge lies not just in understanding these differences, but in leveraging this understanding to build a more just and equitable world. The chapters to follow will delve into the details of specific regions, further enriching this essential comparative exploration of global criminal justice.

1.1 Defining Criminality

Defining criminality proves surprisingly complex, defying simple, universally accepted definitions. What constitutes a crime in one culture might be perfectly acceptable, even expected, behavior in another. This inherent variability stems from deeply ingrained societal values, historical experiences, and evolving moral codes. Consider, for instance, the differing perspectives on theft: in some cultures, sharing resources is a societal norm, making the concept of personal property less defined, thereby altering the perception of theft's severity. In contrast, Western legal systems often place a strong emphasis on individual property rights, consequently classifying theft as a serious crime.

The legal definitions themselves often reflect these cultural nuances. A single act can be classified as a crime in one jurisdiction but a civil matter in another. For example, the concept of "honor killings," considered a serious crime in many Western nations, may have a different legal standing in some parts of the world, reflecting varying cultural interpretations of family honor and justice. This highlights the critical need for a nuanced understanding of the cultural context surrounding any act considered criminal. Ignoring these nuances leads to misinterpretations and ineffective cross-cultural legal cooperation.

Furthermore, the very notion of "criminality" is frequently tied to power structures. Laws are created and enforced by those in power, often reflecting their interests and values. Consequently, acts that challenge the established order might be criminalized, regardless of their inherent morality. Historical examples abound, illustrating how marginalized groups have been disproportionately targeted by laws designed to maintain the status quo. This disparity reveals that what constitutes a crime is not solely a matter of inherent wrongness but also a reflection of prevailing social and political forces. Such considerations make defining "criminality" even more challenging than a simple act versus not an act.

This complex interplay of culture, power, and legal systems underscores the difficulty in establishing a universal definition of criminality. While universal human rights declarations attempt to establish common moral ground, their application and interpretation vary widely across different cultural and legal settings. Indeed, the very concept of "human rights" is itself culturally constructed and interpreted differently across societies. Therefore, any attempt to definitively define "criminality" must acknowledge its contextual nature.

However, despite this inherent variability, some common threads can be identified. Most societies, regardless of their specific cultural norms, criminalize acts that cause significant harm to individuals or society as a whole. These acts often include violence, theft, and fraud. While the specific definitions and penalties may differ, the underlying principle of protecting individuals and maintaining social order remains relatively consistent. This shared concern for the safety and well-being of individuals and society serves as a foundation for cross-cultural dialogue on crime and justice.

Understanding these nuances is crucial for effective cross-cultural cooperation in addressing crime and building more equitable justice systems. Recognizing the impact of cultural factors on the definition and enforcement of laws is the first step towards fostering a more just and globally harmonious world. This awareness, coupled with respectful dialogue, can lead to greater understanding and facilitate the development of more effective, culturally sensitive solutions to global crime issues. Failing to acknowledge these diverse perspectives risks creating ineffective policies and exacerbating existing inequalities. Therefore, effective cross-cultural legal solutions depend on a thorough understanding of these often overlooked and complex considerations. The challenge lies in building bridges between differing legal and cultural frameworks, respecting their unique characteristics while also working towards common goals of justice and social harmony.

1.2 Justice Systems Compared

Diverse societies employ vastly different approaches to justice, reflecting their unique historical, cultural, and social contexts. Western systems, for instance, often prioritize individual rights and due process, employing adversarial legal proceedings with a strong emphasis on precedent in common law traditions. Conversely, many Asian societies favor restorative justice, focusing on reconciliation and reintegration of offenders into the community. This often contrasts sharply with the punitive focus found in many Western legal frameworks, showcasing the range of values that shape how societies deal with crime.

The influence of historical events cannot be overstated. Colonial legacies in Africa, for example, have left an enduring mark on legal systems, creating a complex interplay between traditional dispute resolution mechanisms and the imposed structures of colonial powers. This often results in a hybrid system, attempting to integrate aspects of both, but inevitably facing the challenges of reconciling often conflicting values and priorities. Modern legal reforms often struggle with this duality, needing to address long-standing issues while acknowledging the validity of existing customary practices.

Latin America presents a unique challenge, particularly considering the pervasive influence of the drug trade. This has significantly impacted crime rates and placed immense strain on already fragile judicial systems. The historical context, often shaped by colonial pasts and ingrained inequalities, further complicates the struggle for justice. The region's efforts at legal reform are therefore intertwined with the larger social and economic issues driving criminal activity.

The Middle East presents a nuanced picture. Islamic law's influence varies significantly across different countries, interacting with secular legal frameworks to different degrees. This results in a range of approaches to justice, reflecting the specific cultural and political contexts of each nation. Analyzing these systems requires a careful understanding of the interplay between religious principles and secular governance, recognizing the profound effect of cultural norms on legal processes and outcomes.

Comparing these diverse systems reveals that a single model of justice is neither universally applicable nor desirable. Each system embodies the values and priorities of its society, reflecting its own unique social contract. Understanding these variations requires moving beyond simple comparisons of legal procedures to a deeper engagement with the underlying cultural and philosophical assumptions that shape their application. Effective cross-cultural understanding is paramount, allowing us to appreciate the strengths and limitations of each approach.

The challenge lies in fostering a global dialogue that appreciates these differences while identifying common goals, such as protecting human rights and promoting social justice. International cooperation can play a vital role in this process, fostering exchanges of best practices and collaborative efforts to address transnational crimes. This necessitates a shift from viewing different justice systems as simply distinct entities to recognizing them as valuable sources of insight into how societies grapple with the complex issues of crime and justice.

Effective strategies require careful consideration of cultural sensitivity. A Western-centric approach, for example, might not effectively address issues within a society that prioritizes community harmony. Furthermore, attempts at imposing external models can be counterproductive, failing to account for local contexts and potentially undermining traditional mechanisms of conflict resolution. Therefore, promoting sustainable solutions necessitates a collaborative and culturally sensitive approach.

The study of comparative justice systems provides crucial lessons in adapting and implementing effective crime prevention strategies. Understanding the contextual factors contributing to crime rates allows for developing tailored interventions. For instance, programs aimed at enhancing community cohesion might prove more effective in addressing crime within a restorative justice context, while others focused on individual rehabilitation might find greater success in Western societies.

Ultimately, the diverse approaches to justice highlight the importance of a holistic view. Examining crime rates and considering the legal frameworks in isolation will fall short of understanding the complex interplay between social, economic, and political factors. A comprehensive analysis is required that acknowledges the deep-rooted cultural and historical influences on the perception and response to crime. Only then can we approach the creation of more effective and equitable justice systems.

The comparative study of justice systems isn't just an academic exercise; it has practical implications for creating more just and effective global responses to crime. By understanding the historical, cultural, and social factors shaping different approaches, we can develop more effective strategies for crime prevention and resolution. This understanding allows us to appreciate the limitations of imposing universal standards and encourages a more inclusive approach that values diverse perspectives and practices. Only through respectful engagement and collaboration can we work toward a more just and equitable future.

2 Western Legal Traditions

Western legal traditions, deeply rooted in historical and philosophical contexts, significantly shape how societies define and respond to crime. Understanding these traditions—specifically the common law and civil law systems—is crucial for any comparative study of global justice. Their differences are not merely academic exercises; they manifest in the very structure of legal systems, the roles of judges and juries, and ultimately, in the outcomes of legal proceedings. The contrasts offer invaluable insights into the diverse approaches to justice found around the world.

The common law system, with its origins in England, is characterized by judge-made law. This means that legal principles evolve through judicial decisions, setting precedents that guide future cases. Stare decisis, the principle of respecting precedent, plays a crucial role. It is important to note that this isn't a rigid system. While judges are bound by precedent, they also have the ability to interpret and adapt existing laws to fit the circumstances of a given case. This flexibility allows common law to adapt to evolving societal norms and values over time, but it also introduces an element of unpredictability that is often debated within legal circles. This dynamic interplay between precedent and judicial interpretation is at the core of the common law approach.

In contrast, civil law systems, prevalent in many European and Latin American countries, rely heavily on codified statutes. Comprehensive legal codes serve as the primary source of law, guiding judges in their decisions. While judicial interpretation still plays a role, it's generally less influential than in common law. The focus is on the meticulous application of written laws, creating a system that is often perceived as more predictable but potentially less adaptable to unforeseen circumstances. This structured approach reduces the judicial discretion seen in common law jurisdictions. The importance of thorough codification and its implications on legal interpretation is pivotal to the understanding of civil law approaches.

The role of precedent showcases a key difference between these systems. In common law, precedent is binding on lower courts, creating a hierarchical structure of legal authority. Higher court decisions establish legal principles that must be followed by lower courts in similar cases. This creates a degree of consistency and predictability. In civil law, while past decisions can be influential, they are not legally binding in the same way. Judges are primarily tasked with interpreting and applying existing codified law, leading to a system with a different approach to legal certainty. Therefore, the weight given to precedent reveals the fundamental differences in the structures and goals of these systems.

The interplay between legal theory and practice underscores the complexities of these systems. While the distinctions between common and civil law appear clear in theory, the reality often presents a more nuanced picture. Many jurisdictions blend aspects of both systems, creating hybrid models with unique characteristics. Moreover, within each system, there are diverse interpretations and approaches, influenced by local customs, cultural values, and political considerations. The ongoing evolution and adaptation of legal systems highlights the dynamic interaction of legal principles and societal influences. The practical applica-

tion of legal principles is rarely straightforward, reflecting the inherent complexities of legal systems.
Furthermore, the historical development of these systems is crucial to their current form. The common law evolved organically over centuries, shaped by societal changes and judicial decisions. Civil law systems, often influenced by Roman law, saw periods of formal codification, aiming to create a structured and comprehensive body of law. Understanding their historical development allows us to better understand the core principles and underlying philosophies behind their different approaches. This historical perspective adds crucial context for any assessment of their strengths and weaknesses. The historical development and philosophical influences are critical for a complete picture. This is only a starting point in the broader conversation surrounding comparative legal studies. Understanding these foundational elements lays the groundwork for an exploration of more diverse legal systems found across the globe.

2.1 Common Law Systems

Common law systems, unlike their civil law counterparts, aren't defined by comprehensive, codified statutes. Instead, they rely heavily on precedent—judicial decisions from previous cases that serve as guiding principles for future rulings. This reliance on case law creates a dynamic and ever-evolving legal landscape, shaped by the interpretations of judges and the specific facts of each case. Judges interpret statutes, but also contribute significantly to the development of legal principles through their judgments. The weight given to precedent varies, with some decisions holding more sway than others, based on factors like the court's authority and the longevity of the established principle. This intricate web of precedents, stretching back centuries in some jurisdictions, forms the bedrock of common law. Its flexibility allows for adaptation to changing societal norms and emerging issues, while its adherence to prior decisions promotes consistency and predictability within the legal framework. Understanding this dynamic interplay between precedent and judicial interpretation is crucial to grasping the essence of common law.

The development of common law wasn't a sudden creation, but a gradual process emerging from England's medieval legal practices. Royal judges, traveling throughout the kingdom to administer justice, gradually established a common body of rules and principles, binding across the different regions. Initially, these rules were largely unwritten, transmitted orally and through written records of individual cases. Over time, a system of reporting judicial decisions began to evolve, enabling lawyers and judges to access and rely upon previous rulings. This process, coupled with the increasing professionalization of the legal profession, contributed to the formalization and refinement of common law principles. The influence of equity courts, established to mitigate the perceived harshness of the common law, further enriched its complexity and adaptability.

Stare decisis, the doctrine of precedent, forms the cornerstone of common law methodology. It literally translates to "to stand by things decided," highlighting the importance of adhering to prior judicial rulings. However, the application of stare decisis isn't absolute; judges possess the power to overturn or distinguish previous precedents, particularly if deemed outdated or inapplicable to the current circumstances. This ability to adapt the law is vital for its ongoing relevance in a constantly changing world. The hierarchy of courts further influences the application of precedent, with lower courts generally bound by decisions of higher courts within their jurisdiction. This hierarchical structure ensures some degree of consistency and predictability while allowing for potential modifications and clarifications as cases move up the judicial ladder. Understanding the nuances of stare decisis, and its interplay with judicial discretion, is key to navigating the complexities of common law systems.

One crucial aspect of common law is its adversarial nature. Unlike inquisitorial systems, where the judge plays a more active role in investigating the facts, common law emphasizes the clash of opposing arguments presented by the parties involved. This adversarial process, with its emphasis on cross-examination and the presentation of evidence, is believed to promote a more thorough and rigorous examination of the facts and legal issues in dispute. The judge's role is primarily that of an impartial referee, ensuring a fair trial and applying the relevant legal principles to the evidence presented. The outcome often hinges on the skill of the advocates in presenting their arguments and evidence persuasively. This focus on advocacy, inherent to common law systems, contributes significantly to its perceived robustness and fairness, but also raises potential concerns regarding procedural fairness, especially for those lacking adequate legal representation.

The common law tradition has spread significantly beyond its British origins, influencing legal systems in many countries across the globe, particularly those formerly part of the British Empire. However, the adoption of common law principles hasn't been a uniform process. Many jurisdictions have adapted and modified the system to fit their own unique cultural contexts and legal traditions. This has led to significant variations in how common law operates in different countries, even among those sharing a common historical lineage. For instance, the precise weight given to precedent, the role of judges, and the specific procedural rules can differ considerably. Understanding these variations is critical for anyone seeking to navigate or analyze legal systems influenced by the common law tradition, recognizing it as a constantly evolving global phenomenon shaped by local contexts. This adaptable nature is part of its enduring appeal and resilience, while simultaneously highlighting the complexities of applying common law principles in diverse societal settings.

2.2 Civil Law Systems

Civil law systems, unlike their common law counterparts, derive their authority primarily from codified statutes and legislation. These comprehensive legal codes, meticulously crafted and regularly updated, serve as the cornerstone of the legal framework, providing detailed rules and procedures for resolving disputes. Judges, therefore, play a more interpretative role, applying existing laws to specific cases rather than creating new precedents through judicial decisions. This structured approach offers a degree of predictability and consistency absent in the more fluid evolution of common law. The reliance on codified law often results in a more formalized and structured judicial process, with a greater emphasis on written submissions and evidence.

In contrast to the adversarial nature of common law systems, civil law procedures often incorporate inquisitorial elements. Judges actively investigate the facts of the case, questioning witnesses and seeking evidence to reach a fair and impartial decision. This active role of the judge ensures that all relevant information is considered before judgment is delivered. This contrasts markedly with common law systems where the opposing parties bear the primary responsibility for presenting evidence and arguments. The inquisitorial approach, however, can sometimes be perceived as less transparent to the parties involved in the legal proceedings.

The concept of precedent, a cornerstone of common law, holds significantly less weight in civil law systems. While past judicial decisions may offer guidance, they are not binding in the same way as in common law jurisdictions. The emphasis remains firmly on the application of the codified law, ensuring consistency across different courts and judgments. This focus on the written law, however, may lead to a certain rigidity in adapting to evolving societal norms and values. Changes to the law require legislative action rather than organic development through judicial interpretation.

Training for judges and lawyers in civil law systems differs substantially. A strong emphasis is placed on thorough legal scholarship and the ability to meticulously interpret and apply the codified law. Law schools generally focus on intensive study of legal codes and doctrines, preparing students for the role of legal interpreters rather than the adversarial advocates often found in common law training. The theoretical understanding of the legal framework is paramount, equipping legal professionals with the tools for accurate and consistent application of existing laws.

However, despite the codified nature of civil law, some flexibility exists. While judges aren't creating binding precedent, their interpretations of the code can still subtly influence future decisions. Furthermore, the way the code is applied can vary based on context and the specific wording within the code itself, making it less rigid than it might appear initially. Furthermore, many civil law jurisdictions incorporate elements of other legal traditions, resulting in hybrid systems that reflect a more nuanced and complex reality.

The role of legal scholars in civil law systems is particularly crucial. Their analyses of the code, their commentary on its application, and their contributions to legal literature inform judicial interpretations and legislative reforms. This highlights the importance of legal scholarship in shaping and clarifying the meaning of the codified law itself. The interplay between legal scholarship, legislative action, and judicial interpretation constitutes a dynamic process that continually shapes the evolution of civil law systems.

While the systematic approach of civil law offers predictability and consistency, it can also create challenges. The codified nature of the law can struggle to keep pace with rapid societal changes, occasionally leading to laws becoming outdated or inadequate in addressing contemporary issues. This can require significant legislative intervention to amend or update the codified statutes, necessitating a potentially lengthy and complex process. The rigid structure, while offering clarity, can sometimes stifle innovative solutions to unique legal problems.

In summary, civil law systems, rooted in codified statutes and judicial interpretation, offer a distinct alternative to common law traditions. Their emphasis on codified law, inquisitorial procedures, and the limited influence of precedent contribute to a unique legal landscape. Understanding these characteristics is essential for navigating the complexities of international legal frameworks and appreciating the diverse approaches to justice around the world. The interplay between codified law, judicial interpretation, and legal scholarship ultimately defines the dynamism and adaptability of civil law systems globally. The inherent strengths and weaknesses of this approach are continually shaped by societal needs and legal reforms.

2.3 The Role of Precedent

The concept of precedent, a cornerstone of common law systems, significantly shapes legal interpretations and judicial decisions. It's a principle based on the idea that similar cases should be decided similarly, ensuring consistency and predictability within the legal framework. This reliance on past rulings, however, doesn't imply rigid inflexibility. Judges carefully consider the specific facts of each case, comparing them to previous precedents to identify similarities and differences. The weight given to a precedent varies depending on the court's hierarchy and the precedent's age, with higher courts' decisions holding more sway than those of lower courts, and more recent decisions often carrying greater weight than older ones. This dynamic interaction between established precedent and the unique details of new cases creates a complex and evolving body of law. The interpretation and application of precedent require nuanced judgment and a deep understanding of legal history.

Understanding the hierarchical nature of precedent is crucial. Decisions from higher courts, like Supreme Courts, are binding on lower courts within the same jurisdiction. This means lower courts must follow the rulings of higher courts on similar issues. However, lower courts have the flexibility to distinguish cases, arguing that the facts differ sufficiently to warrant a different outcome. This ability to distinguish cases allows for the legal system to adapt to changing circumstances and societal norms, preventing the rigid application of outdated precedents. It's a delicate balance, though; judges must carefully justify their distinctions, ensuring that the deviations from established precedent are well-reasoned and supported by relevant legal arguments. The process, therefore, is not simply a mechanical application of rules, but a considered judgment call.

The doctrine of stare decisis, Latin for "to stand by things decided," underpins the principle of precedent. It reflects the common law's emphasis on stability and predictability. By relying on past decisions, stare decisis fosters consistency and ensures that similar cases are treated similarly, fostering fairness and reducing uncertainty. Individuals and businesses can rely on established legal principles to guide their actions, knowing that the courts will generally adhere to consistent interpretations of the law. However, stare decisis is not absolute. Courts can overturn previous precedents if they are deemed to be incorrect or no longer reflective of societal values or evolving legal principles. This is particularly important in addressing social injustice or adapting the law to changing technologies or social norms. Overturning precedent, though, is not taken lightly and generally requires compelling reasons to justify such a significant departure from established legal norms.

The use of precedent, however, presents certain challenges. Firstly, the sheer volume of case law can be overwhelming, making it difficult for legal professionals to find and apply relevant precedents. The constant expansion of case law requires sophisticated legal research and effective database management to allow professionals to navigate the vast body of judgments to uncover those genuinely relevant to the cases in hand. This issue is exacerbated by the fact that case law often develops incrementally, with judges building upon and refining existing precedents over time. Secondly, the language used in judgments can be complex and ambiguous, leading to varied interpretations. This ambiguity creates difficulties in applying precedents to new cases and necessitates careful analysis and consideration of the specific circumstances of each case, requiring significant levels of expertise. Consequently, achieving uniform application of precedent across different courts can prove remarkably challenging.

The role of precedent is particularly significant in areas where legislation is sparse or ambiguous. In such instances, judicial decisions based on precedent can fill in the gaps, clarifying the law and providing guidance to individuals and organizations. This proactive role of the judiciary helps to resolve uncertainty and promotes greater certainty in the legal landscape. Moreover, precedent can help courts adapt the law to new situations and emerging technologies, thereby ensuring that legal frameworks remain relevant and effective in a constantly evolving world. However, this adaptable quality of precedent necessitates a cautious approach to avoid inconsistencies and maintain a coherent and stable legal framework, constantly balancing established norms with the need to address new and unique situations. A delicate balance is struck, ensuring legal progress without sacrificing predictability. The judicial process must navigate this complexity with great care.

3 Asian Perspectives on Crime

Many Asian societies, particularly those influenced by Confucianism, prioritize social harmony and the restoration of relationships damaged by crime, rather than solely focusing on punishment. This emphasis on restoring balance within the community contrasts sharply with Western legal traditions that often prioritize retribution. The concept of "face," crucial in many Asian cultures, significantly impacts how crimes are perceived and addressed. Losing face can be a powerful deterrent, motivating individuals to avoid actions that might bring shame upon themselves and their families. This emphasis on social standing acts as a form of informal social control.

Restorative justice practices, common in several Asian countries, exemplify this focus on reconciliation. These practices often involve bringing together the victim, offender, and community members to find a resolution that addresses the harm caused and repairs the damaged relationships. Mediation and negotiation play central roles, aiming for a mutually agreeable outcome that emphasizes healing and reintegration into society, instead of simply imprisoning the offender. Such processes are deeply embedded in the cultural understanding of justice and its role in maintaining social cohesion. The effectiveness of restorative justice, however, depends on the specific cultural context and the willingness of all parties to participate actively in the process. Challenges remain, particularly in cases involving serious violent crimes or where power imbalances between victim and offender significantly hinder equitable resolution.

For instance, in some parts of Japan, community-based dispute resolution mechanisms have existed for centuries. These mechanisms, often relying on informal mediation and reconciliation, prioritize maintaining social harmony and resolving conflicts outside of the formal court system. The emphasis is on preventing escalation and maintaining community peace, rather than on adversarial legal proceedings and subsequent incarceration. This aligns with the Confucian emphasis on social order and the importance of maintaining respectful relationships. However, the effectiveness of these systems can be questioned when faced with complex or highly emotional disputes. Furthermore, the extent to which they successfully address the needs of victims and ensure accountability for offenders remains a topic of ongoing debate and research.

Unlike Western legal systems that emphasize codified laws and strict adherence to legal procedure, several Asian legal systems incorporate elements of flexibility and discretion. Judges often consider the specific circumstances of a case and the potential impact on the community when making decisions. This approach, while potentially leading to inconsistent outcomes, reflects the cultural emphasis on context and the desire to achieve just outcomes based on the unique details of each situation. This contextual approach aligns with the understanding of justice as a dynamic process rather than a rigid application of abstract legal principles. This flexibility, while potentially creating uneven application of the law, reflects the cultural prioritization of achieving practical solutions that maintain social harmony.

The influence of Confucianism is particularly evident in the emphasis on education and rehabilitation within the Asian criminal justice system. The focus is not only on punishing offenders but also on helping them to reintegrate into society and become productive members of the community. This perspective reflects a belief in the potential for redemption and the importance of fostering social responsibility. The use of community service and restorative justice programs demonstrates a commitment to rehabilitation and reintegration as crucial aspects of the justice process. This emphasis, however, doesn't imply a lack of punitive measures, as appropriate sanctions remain a part of the justice system. The balance between punishment and rehabilitation, however, often differs significantly from Western approaches.

The concept of shame and honor also profoundly affects how crimes are viewed and dealt with in numerous Asian cultures. The potential for shame associated with criminal behavior can act as a powerful deterrent, prompting individuals to act responsibly and avoid actions that could harm their reputation and their family's standing within the community. The social pressure to maintain a positive image and avoid dishonor can significantly influence behavior. This emphasis on social standing creates a form of informal social control that supplements, and in some cases, replaces, the need for strict formal legal sanctions. However, this system is not without its flaws and can be particularly difficult for individuals from marginalized groups or those already facing social stigma.

Furthermore, the level of government involvement and the influence of community-based solutions vary across different Asian countries. Some jurisdictions maintain strong centralized criminal justice systems, while others utilize more decentralized, community-oriented approaches. This variation reflects the diversity of cultural traditions and legal systems across the Asian continent. Understanding these variations requires a nuanced understanding of specific cultural and legal contexts, moving beyond simplistic generalizations. Detailed research and case studies are necessary to fully grasp the complexities and specificities of crime and justice in different Asian nations. The range of practices highlights that a universal Asian approach to crime and justice does not exist. Instead, there is a spectrum of responses, all sharing certain underlying principles while differing significantly in implementation.

3.1 Confucian Influences

Confucian philosophy, deeply ingrained in East Asian societies for millennia, profoundly shapes perceptions of crime and justice. Unlike Western systems that often prioritize individual rights and retribution, Confucianism emphasizes social harmony and the restoration of relationships damaged by criminal acts. This emphasis on collective well-being, rather than individual punishment, fundamentally alters the approach to crime prevention and resolution. The core tenets of Confucianism - ren (benevolence), yi (righteousness), li (ritual propriety), and zhi (wisdom) - provide a framework for understanding this distinct perspective. Crimes are not merely violations of the law but disruptions to the social fabric, requiring restoration rather than solely punishment.

The concept of li, or ritual propriety, plays a crucial role. Adherence to social norms and expectations is paramount; deviations are viewed as not only legal infractions but also moral failures that disrupt social order. This perspective encourages preventative measures, focusing on education and social conditioning to foster adherence to li and minimize criminal behavior. Instead of solely relying on punitive measures, Confucian principles emphasize rehabilitation and reintegration into society. Restorative justice practices, which prioritize reconciliation and repair between offenders and victims, align seamlessly with this philosophy. These practices aim to mend damaged relationships and restore social harmony, mitigating the need for harsh punishments that might exacerbate societal divisions.

Unlike Western adversarial systems, where the focus is on establishing guilt or innocence through confrontation, Confucian-influenced approaches often prioritize mediation and negotiation. This emphasis on consensus-building allows for solutions tailored to specific contexts, acknowledging the complexities of human relationships and the nuanced nature of wrongdoing. The goal isn't simply to punish but to restore balance and harmony within the community. For instance, community mediation and restorative justice programs, frequently implemented in East Asian societies, reflect this emphasis on collaboration and mutual understanding. These programs often involve not only the offender and victim but also community members, facilitating dialogue, and fostering a collective sense of responsibility for restoring social order.

Furthermore, Confucianism emphasizes the importance of education and moral development in preventing crime. The cultivation of virtues like ren (benevolence) and yi (righteousness) is seen as crucial to creating a just and harmonious society. Thus, investment in education and character development is considered a vital component of crime prevention strategies. This holistic approach contrasts sharply with Western approaches, which often focus more heavily on law enforcement and punishment. This difference in emphasis reflects contrasting values: while Western systems tend to prioritize individual responsibility and the protection of individual rights, Confucianism stresses social responsibility and the preservation of communal harmony.

However, it's important to acknowledge the complexities of applying Confucian principles in modern contexts. Rapid modernization and globalization have introduced new challenges, necessitating adaptations to traditional approaches. Issues like economic inequality, technological advancements, and transnational crime require innovative solutions that incorporate elements of both traditional and modern justice systems. While restorative justice and mediation remain valuable tools, they aren't always sufficient to address complex or severe crimes. Balancing the emphasis on harmony with the need for justice and accountability is a continual challenge that requires a nuanced approach. Striking this balance requires careful consideration of the specific circumstances of each case, recognizing the limitations of relying solely on traditional models in a rapidly changing world. The evolving nature of crime and the increasing interconnectedness of societies demand a continuous reassessment and adaptation of legal and judicial approaches, even within the context of deeply rooted philosophical traditions such as Confucianism. The ongoing challenge is to preserve the core values of harmony and social responsibility while addressing the demands of a complex and dynamic global landscape. This delicate balance forms the crux of contemporary debates on justice within Confucian-influenced societies.

3.2 Restorative Justice Models

Many Asian societies, particularly those influenced by Confucian philosophies, prioritize harmony and social order above all else. This emphasis shapes their approaches to justice, leading to a strong preference for restorative justice models. Unlike Western systems that often focus on punishment and retribution, these models aim to repair harm caused by crime and restore relationships between the offender, victim, and community. This isn't simply about avoiding punishment; it's a fundamentally different approach to justice, one that prioritizes reconciliation and reintegration.

Restorative justice in these contexts often involves bringing together the offender, victim, and relevant community members in a mediated dialogue. The goal is not to determine guilt or innocence in a formal setting, but to facilitate a process where the offender takes responsibility for their actions, the victim has an opportunity to express their pain and needs, and the community can work collectively to heal the harm. This process can involve apologies, restitution, community service, and other measures designed to address the specific needs of all involved parties. Think of it as a collaborative problem-solving exercise focused on repairing damaged relationships and restoring social harmony.

The success of restorative justice initiatives depends heavily on the active participation of all stakeholders. The process demands a high level of trust and transparency, requiring skilled mediators who can navigate complex emotional dynamics and ensure a fair and respectful environment. The community's role is crucial—it's not merely an observer, but an active participant in the healing process, providing support and accountability to both the offender and the victim. This community involvement often distinguishes restorative practices from traditional Western approaches where the state assumes primary responsibility for justice.

Critically, the effectiveness of restorative justice isn't solely measured by the absence of recidivism, although that's certainly an important factor. It's also measured by its impact on repairing relationships, fostering community healing, and promoting a sense of collective responsibility. While empirical evidence supporting restorative justice's effectiveness varies across studies and contexts, a significant body of research suggests that when properly implemented, these models can lead to lower recidivism rates and improved victim satisfaction compared to purely punitive approaches.

However, restorative justice isn't a panacea. It's not suitable for all types of crimes, and its implementation can face challenges. For instance, serious violent crimes might necessitate a more formal legal process, while cultural sensitivities and power imbalances can hinder successful mediation. Furthermore, ensuring equal access to restorative justice services for all members of the community, regardless of their social status or background, poses a significant challenge. Effective implementation requires careful consideration of these limitations, robust training for mediators, and ongoing evaluation to assess its efficacy and make necessary adaptations. The context is key; it's not a one-size-fits-all solution.

One significant difference from Western systems lies in the concept of shame and honor. In some Asian cultures, shame plays a crucial role in social control. The prospect of losing face within the community can be a powerful deterrent, and restorative justice processes often leverage this to encourage offenders to take responsibility and repair the harm they've caused. Reintegration back into the community, therefore, isn't just a matter of legal compliance; it's a deeply social and cultural process with significant implications for the individual's standing within their social circle.

The integration of restorative justice models with formal legal systems presents another area of complexity. Many Asian societies are navigating the process of integrating traditional restorative practices with modern legal frameworks inherited from colonial periods. This necessitates careful consideration of how to balance the principles of fairness, accountability, and community healing within a structured legal environment. The challenge lies in finding a balance that respects traditional customs while ensuring compliance with modern legal standards and protecting the rights of victims.

Finally, research into restorative justice practices in Asia is ongoing, and much remains to be understood. While the principles are broadly applicable, the specific methods and their effectiveness vary significantly across different cultures and communities. Further research is needed to understand better the factors that contribute to successful implementation, to address the challenges involved, and to evaluate the long-term impacts of these models on crime rates, victim well-being, and community cohesion. It is imperative to approach the study of these practices with sensitivity and respect for cultural contexts. This ongoing scholarship will be crucial to refining and expanding the use of restorative justice to promote a fairer and more harmonious society.

4 African Approaches to Justice

Many African societies have long-standing traditions of conflict resolution that predate formal legal systems. These customary practices often prioritize mediation, negotiation, and reconciliation, aiming to restore harmony within the community rather than solely punishing offenders. Family and community elders frequently play crucial roles in these processes, leveraging their knowledge of social dynamics and relationships to facilitate agreement. The emphasis is on restoring balance and repairing social fabric, a stark contrast to the adversarial nature of many Western legal systems. Restorative justice principles are deeply embedded in these traditional approaches, highlighting the importance of community involvement and repairing harm caused by criminal acts. These methods, while effective in many contexts, face challenges in the modern era, especially with regard to addressing complex crimes and ensuring consistent application of justice. The arrival of colonial powers significantly altered the legal landscapes of many African nations. European legal systems, primarily based on common or civil law traditions, were imposed, often overriding or suppressing existing customary practices. This imposition led to a complex interplay between traditional and colonial legal frameworks, creating a hybrid system that continues to shape legal realities today. Many existing customary laws were codified into modern legal systems, often resulting in a blending of indigenous and colonial approaches. The legacy of colonialism is pervasive and continues to influence law enforcement, judicial processes, and the perceptions of justice. The effects of this lasting colonial legacy manifest in issues like institutional inequities, limited resources, and a lack of cultural sensitivity within the legal systems.

Post-colonial Africa has witnessed significant legal reforms aimed at modernizing and adapting legal systems to contemporary challenges. These reforms often involve incorporating international human rights standards and adapting legal frameworks to address issues such as gender equality, human trafficking, and corruption. However, the pace of reform varies considerably across the continent, with many nations struggling to implement effective legal frameworks. The challenge lies in harmonizing traditional practices with modern legal structures, balancing the need for consistency with the need for cultural sensitivity. These processes often need extensive engagement with local communities, ensuring that reforms align with local values while upholding international standards.

Community-based justice initiatives have gained traction in recent years as a way to address the limitations of formal legal systems and to integrate traditional approaches within contemporary frameworks. These initiatives emphasize participatory justice, involving community members in resolving disputes and addressing criminal behavior. They often rely on restorative justice principles, focusing on repairing harm and reintegrating offenders into the community. However, such initiatives face significant challenges, including access to resources, training, and overcoming deeply entrenched power imbalances and societal biases. Success frequently depends on the ability to secure community buy-in and sustainable funding, and this success is not consistently realized across different communities.

The successful adaptation of legal systems in Africa requires a delicate balance between upholding the rule of law and recognizing the value of diverse cultural contexts. Challenges include addressing issues of access to justice, corruption, and limited resources, alongside the persistent tension between traditional and modern legal approaches. This constant negotiation between tradition and modernity requires careful consideration of cultural sensitivity, the avoidance of further marginalization, and continuous evaluation of legal reforms. Building strong, equitable and culturally relevant legal systems necessitates a participatory approach that values the involvement of affected communities, fostering a genuine sense of justice.

4.1 Traditional Dispute Resolution

Many African societies, prior to significant European influence, relied on intricate systems of traditional dispute resolution. These weren't formalized court systems in the Western sense; instead, they often involved community elders, chiefs, or other respected figures mediating conflicts. The emphasis was firmly on restoring harmony within the community, rather than simply punishing offenders. These processes frequently incorporated customary law, passed down through generations, shaping the understanding of justice and fairness. The specifics varied wildly, reflecting the remarkable diversity across the African continent. Some communities might utilize storytelling or symbolic actions to address wrongs; others may lean on more structured processes involving oaths, ordeals, or even forms of arbitration. The key element remained the prioritization of reconciliation and community cohesion.

These traditional methods often integrated restorative justice principles long before the concept gained international recognition. Instead of focusing solely on retribution, the goal was to repair relationships damaged by conflict. Offenders were frequently expected to make amends to victims, and the community played a vital role in facilitating this process. This holistic approach, addressing both the harm caused and the needs of the community, significantly differed from the adversarial nature of many Western legal systems. The community's collective responsibility extended beyond the immediate parties involved, emphasizing the interconnectedness of social life and the importance of maintaining order through shared values. The emphasis on social harmony meant that the success of a dispute resolution process wasn't solely measured by legal outcomes but by the restoration of peace and the prevention of future conflicts. This community-centred approach to justice has profound implications for contemporary discussions of restorative justice, offering valuable insights and potential models for more inclusive and effective conflict resolution strategies globally.

However, the colonial era profoundly impacted traditional dispute resolution systems across Africa. The imposition of European legal systems often marginalized or outright suppressed indigenous practices, leading to a complex interplay between customary and formal legal frameworks. This created a power imbalance, favoring the colonial legal system, often overlooking and dismissing the legitimacy and value of established customary traditions. The introduction of Western legal concepts, such as codified laws and formal court procedures, fundamentally altered the way disputes were handled and often undermined the effectiveness of traditional mechanisms that had worked for generations. Many communities experienced the erosion of their cultural heritage and the disruption of their social structures as a result. These lasting impacts continue to shape contemporary legal landscapes in many African nations, leading to ongoing discussions about integrating aspects of traditional practices into modern legal frameworks.

Despite the challenges posed by colonial legacies and the complexities of modernization, many African communities continue to utilize aspects of traditional dispute resolution systems. These systems often function in parallel with formal legal processes, offering alternative pathways for resolving conflicts, particularly at the community level. They maintain a strong emphasis on mediation and negotiation, often involving community elders and other respected figures to facilitate dialogue and reach agreements acceptable to all parties involved. Their persistence demonstrates the enduring relevance and resilience of these traditional practices, reflecting a continued preference for community-based approaches to conflict resolution. Furthermore, they highlight the valuable role that local customs and traditional knowledge can play in addressing contemporary societal challenges. This continued reliance on traditional systems underscores a profound need to consider the cultural context when implementing legal reforms in Africa.

The integration of traditional dispute resolution mechanisms into contemporary legal frameworks poses significant challenges. One major hurdle is the need to reconcile customary law with codified legal systems. This requires careful consideration of potential conflicts between traditional practices and modern legal principles. Moreover, ensuring fairness, transparency, and accountability within traditional processes is crucial to maintain public trust and confidence. Striking a balance between preserving cultural heritage and upholding contemporary standards of justice demands sensitivity, inclusivity, and thoughtful legal reform. The process needs to account for the diversity of customary practices across the continent, while simultaneously addressing issues like gender inequality, power imbalances, and the risk of marginalization within certain traditional processes. Therefore, any attempt at integration requires careful and nuanced approaches, tailored to the specific contexts and complexities of each community.

4.2 Colonial Legal Impacts

The legacy of colonialism profoundly shaped African legal systems, leaving an enduring impact on how crime is defined and justice administered. European powers, during their periods of dominance, often imposed their own legal frameworks, disregarding existing indigenous practices and customary laws. This imposition frequently resulted in the suppression of traditional dispute resolution methods, mechanisms often deeply embedded within community structures and designed for restorative justice, focusing on reconciliation and community healing rather than solely punishment. The introduction of Western legal concepts, such as codified statutes, adversarial proceedings, and formal court systems, sometimes clashed directly with existing cultural norms and values.

This imposition of foreign legal systems created inherent tensions. Many traditional African societies relied on community-based conflict resolution, involving elders, chiefs, and community members to mediate disputes and restore harmony. These methods, often rooted in strong social ties and shared cultural understanding, fostered a sense of collective responsibility and accountability. By contrast, the formal Western legal systems introduced a hierarchical structure, distancing justice from the community and potentially alienating those most affected by crime. This shift often marginalized indigenous knowledge and expertise, impacting local participation in legal proceedings and undermining community trust in the justice system.

Furthermore, colonial legal systems often served to reinforce existing power imbalances. Laws were frequently implemented to regulate and control colonial subjects, rather than to address their needs. Land ownership, taxation, and labor laws, for example, were often structured in ways that benefited colonial interests, dispossessing local communities and perpetuating economic inequalities. This created a deeply ingrained sense of injustice and mistrust, shaping the perception of the legal system as an instrument of oppression rather than a vehicle for fairness and equity. These historical injustices continue to shape modern legal challenges in many African nations.

The consequences of colonial legal legacies are complex and multifaceted. In some instances, elements of traditional and customary law have survived, coexisting alongside formal legal systems. In other cases, a complete replacement of indigenous legal structures occurred, leaving a void in community-based dispute resolution. The resulting legal landscape is often characterized by a combination of formal and informal justice mechanisms, which frequently operate in parallel but sometimes in conflict. This creates challenges in achieving consistent and equitable outcomes. Navigating this duality requires careful consideration of cultural context, legal history, and the needs of local communities.

The enduring impact of colonialism necessitates a nuanced understanding of modern African legal systems. Simple analyses risk ignoring the intricate interplay between traditional and imported legal frameworks. Recognizing the inherent contradictions and tensions within these hybrid systems is crucial for effective legal reform and the pursuit of justice. Indeed, it's necessary to acknowledge the lasting effects of colonialism on perceptions of law and authority, shaping not just the formal legal structure but also societal attitudes toward the justice system. This historical context provides a critical lens through which to examine modern challenges and to design legal interventions that truly serve the needs of African communities. Understanding this history is essential for fostering sustainable and equitable justice systems that uphold both the rule of law and cultural integrity. Only through acknowledging and addressing these historical imbalances can we hope to build truly just and equitable societies. The path toward this goal requires a commitment to inclusive legal reform, mindful of both the benefits of modern legal frameworks and the enduring value of traditional dispute resolution methods. It necessitates the active participation of local communities in the design and implementation of legal reforms, ensuring that the justice system reflects the values and needs of the people it serves. The road ahead involves constant adaptation, balancing the demands of modern legal challenges with the resilience and wisdom of traditional African legal practices.

4.3 Modern Legal Reforms

Many African nations grapple with outdated legal frameworks inherited from colonial rule. These systems often fail to address the unique needs and contexts of their communities, leading to persistent injustices. Modernization efforts must therefore prioritize aligning legal structures with local customs and realities, while simultaneously ensuring adherence to international human rights standards. This delicate balancing act requires careful consideration of existing traditions and the potential for unintended consequences. Successful reform necessitates inclusive participation from local communities, fostering ownership and buy-in from those most affected.

The incorporation of traditional dispute resolution mechanisms into formal legal systems presents a significant opportunity for progress. These age-old practices, often rooted in community consensus and restorative justice principles, can offer more effective and culturally sensitive solutions to certain types of conflict. Integration, however, requires careful planning to avoid undermining the rule of law or perpetuating harmful traditional practices. For example, some traditional practices might discriminate against specific groups, while others might conflict with international norms protecting human rights. Thus, selective integration—choosing compatible practices and amending conflicting ones—is critical. This process requires extensive research, consultation with communities, and close monitoring to ensure fairness and effectiveness.

Furthermore, modern legal reforms in Africa must address the capacity constraints within judicial systems. Many nations lack sufficient resources, personnel, and infrastructure to effectively administer justice. Addressing this requires targeted investments in judicial training, infrastructure improvements, and the creation of supportive legal environments. This includes initiatives to reduce case backlogs, increase access to legal aid, and improve the efficiency of court processes. Improved training is crucial in enhancing legal expertise and promotes adherence to international legal standards. Simultaneously, advancements in technology can help streamline court procedures and increase access to justice, but only when implemented alongside substantial investments in infrastructure and personnel. It requires a holistic approach.

Moreover, the issue of corruption within legal systems demands urgent attention. Corruption undermines the rule of law, erodes public trust, and perpetuates inequality. Addressing this requires enacting and enforcing robust anti-corruption laws, combined with public awareness campaigns to foster a culture of accountability. International cooperation can play a crucial role in assisting nations in developing transparent and effective anti-corruption strategies. This cooperation might involve sharing best practices, providing technical assistance, and fostering regional collaborations. Ultimately, curbing corruption demands a multi-pronged approach involving legislative reforms, institutional strengthening, and a commitment to ethical conduct within all aspects of the legal system.

Critically, legal reforms must also address the persistent challenges of gender inequality within the justice system. Many African societies still face deeply entrenched patriarchal structures, resulting in discriminatory practices within the legal system itself. Modernizing laws requires a focus on ensuring equal access to justice for all, regardless of gender. This includes enacting legislation explicitly prohibiting gender-based violence, providing specialized support services for victims, and promoting the representation of women in all aspects of the legal profession. Progress requires not just legal changes, but also broader societal shifts in attitudes and behaviors. Education and awareness campaigns targeting societal norms play a critical role in achieving lasting change. The inclusion of women in decision-making processes at all levels is equally important, both in the legislature and the judiciary.

Finally, effective legal reforms must be sustainable. They must be integrated into the existing legal and social fabric of each nation, ensuring that they resonate with the local context and are capable of long-term impact. This requires ongoing monitoring and evaluation to assess their effectiveness and adapt them as needed. Sustainability also necessitates empowering local communities to participate actively in shaping and implementing legal reforms, fostering a sense of ownership and shared responsibility for the justice system's success. Continuous evaluation and community engagement are critical to adapting legal frameworks to evolving social and economic circumstances. Only by actively engaging with communities can lasting and impactful legal reforms become a reality in Africa.

4.4 Community-Based Justice

Community-based justice, in the African context, often represents a fascinating blend of traditional practices and modern legal frameworks. It's not simply a replacement for formal court systems, but rather a crucial supplement, often handling disputes more effectively and efficiently than overburdened courts. Its success depends heavily on the active involvement of community members, acting as mediators, conciliators, and restorative agents— roles that empower individuals and strengthen societal bonds. This differs significantly from the formal, adversarial processes seen in Western legal systems, where the focus is often on assigning blame and administering punishment. The emphasis shifts from retribution to reconciliation. This nuanced approach prioritizes repairing harm to both the victim and the community. The effectiveness of community-based justice is profoundly tied to the specific cultural context. Traditional African societies frequently utilize customary law, a body of rules and practices passed down through generations, to resolve conflicts. These customary mechanisms are deeply ingrained in the social fabric and often hold more weight than formal laws in many communities. Understanding this intricate relationship between custom and formal law is essential for comprehending how community-based justice actually functions and where its greatest strengths lie. Ignoring the intricate tapestry of societal customs can lead to ineffective or even counterproductive outcomes. The integration of traditional practices into modern legal processes is not just an academic pursuit, it's a practical necessity for meaningful justice. Consider the role of elders in many African communities. They are often revered for their wisdom and experience, serving as respected figures capable of mediating disputes fairly and effectively. Their involvement goes beyond simple conflict resolution; their actions build community trust and help maintain social harmony. Their decisions are typically based on community consensus, fostering a sense of collective responsibility and ownership of the outcome. This contrasts starkly with the often impersonal nature of formal court proceedings in many other legal systems. The personal touch of community-based justice, though reliant on individual community members, has proven successful in many parts of Africa.

However, implementing and maintaining community-based justice systems presents inherent challenges. One significant hurdle is the need for consistent training and support for community leaders and mediators. Effective conflict resolution requires specific skills, including active listening, empathy, and negotiation techniques. Without adequate training, the potential for bias, unfair decisions, and community discord significantly increases. Further compounding the challenges is the risk of cultural clashes arising from the interaction between traditional customary practices and the imposition of modern legal codes inherited from colonial legacies. These factors often require ongoing adaptation, and navigating this delicate balance is crucial for success.

Furthermore, community-based justice cannot be a stand-alone solution. It needs support from the formal legal system, which must be equipped to handle cases that fall outside the scope of community resolution, such as serious crimes or those requiring specialized legal expertise. This requires collaboration and clear communication between the community and the formal justice system, recognizing the vital roles each plays. The lack of clear lines of demarcation can lead to confusion and undermine the credibility of the process. Collaboration between the state and the community is crucial, and this must be fostered through funding, training, and technical support. Without this, community-based justice initiatives risk becoming unsustainable and ineffective.

The integration of community-based justice into modern legal frameworks requires a careful and nuanced approach. It's not a simple matter of replacing existing structures; instead, it involves creating a complementary system that leverages the strengths of traditional practices while addressing the limitations of formal justice. Successful implementation demands ongoing evaluation, adaptation, and a commitment to fostering collaboration between community leaders, legal professionals, and policymakers. This collaborative approach, built on mutual respect and understanding, creates a synergy that promotes effective and equitable justice. It is a dynamic and evolving system, continually adapted to meet the unique needs of each community. Ultimately, its success relies on an approach that respects tradition, embraces modern best practices, and fosters a deep sense of community participation and responsibility.

4.5 Challenges and Adaptations

The challenges facing African legal systems are multifaceted and deeply intertwined with historical, social, and economic factors. Colonial legacies, for example, imposed legal frameworks often ill-suited to existing customary practices, creating a complex interplay of traditional and imposed laws. This has led to inconsistencies and sometimes outright conflicts in the application of justice, leaving many communities feeling alienated from the legal process. The resulting lack of trust in formal legal institutions frequently drives individuals to rely on traditional dispute resolution mechanisms, which, while possessing inherent value, may lack the capacity to address complex modern crimes. Furthermore, limited resources, inadequate infrastructure, and a shortage of trained legal professionals exacerbate these issues, hindering the effective implementation of even well-intended legal reforms. This necessitates a nuanced approach, respecting the value of existing community structures while simultaneously building capacity within the formal legal system to address contemporary challenges effectively.

Resource limitations profoundly impact the ability of African nations to effectively combat crime and administer justice. Many countries struggle with inadequate funding for law enforcement agencies, leading to understaffing, poor equipment, and limited investigative capabilities. Similarly, judicial systems often face backlogs of cases, lengthy delays in trials, and a lack of access to legal representation, particularly for marginalized communities. This creates a system where justice is slow, inefficient, and often inaccessible to those who need it most. The absence of adequate prisons and rehabilitation facilities also contributes to recidivism, undermining efforts to reduce crime rates effectively. Addressing this requires a significant investment in infrastructure, training, and technology, alongside broader societal reforms aimed at improving governance and reducing inequality.

Modern legal reforms in Africa often grapple with the complexities of balancing the need for modernization with the preservation of traditional values. The introduction of Western-style legal systems has frequently resulted in tensions between formal laws and customary practices, creating a situation where individuals may find themselves navigating two distinct, often conflicting, legal frameworks. This can lead to confusion, inconsistency, and a lack of clarity in the application of the law. Reconciling these differences requires careful consideration of local customs, traditions, and social contexts. Integrating aspects of traditional dispute resolution into modern legal systems, while also upholding standards of fairness and due process, presents a significant challenge that demands innovative approaches and a deep understanding of the cultural landscape.

Furthermore, the rise of transnational crime, including drug trafficking, human trafficking, and cybercrime, poses significant challenges to African countries' efforts to maintain law and order. These crimes often transcend national borders, requiring regional and international cooperation to effectively combat them. This necessitates strengthening regional collaborations, developing sophisticated intelligence-sharing mechanisms, and fostering a coordinated response among affected nations. It also calls for enhanced capacity building in law enforcement agencies and judicial institutions to address the specific challenges posed by these increasingly sophisticated forms of criminal activity. Adapting to this evolving landscape demands constant innovation and proactive engagement with international partners.

Community-based justice initiatives are gaining traction as a means of addressing the challenges of limited resources and building trust in legal institutions. By engaging local communities in the administration of justice, these initiatives seek to improve accessibility, promote restorative justice practices, and foster a sense of ownership over the legal process. Successful implementation requires active participation from community members, careful consideration of local customs, and robust mechanisms for accountability and oversight. However, the effectiveness of community-based justice initiatives depends heavily on the specific context and may not be suitable for all types of crime. A careful evaluation of their effectiveness is essential to ensure their sustainability and impact. The key is to ensure the development of well-structured and responsible initiatives that blend traditional practices with modern legal concepts in a sensible and equitable way.

5 Latin American Crime & Justice

Latin America's complex relationship with crime and justice is deeply rooted in its tumultuous history. Colonialism left a legacy of inequality and instability, creating fertile ground for the proliferation of criminal activities. This wasn't merely the imposition of a new legal system; it was the systematic dismantling of existing social structures and the introduction of economic policies that favored a select few, leaving the vast majority vulnerable to exploitation and marginalization. These historical injustices continue to resonate in the present-day realities of crime and violence.

The drug trade, a particularly pervasive issue, casts a long shadow over many Latin American nations. Its impact extends far beyond simply the trafficking of narcotics. It fuels corruption, influencing law enforcement, judicial processes, and even the political landscape itself. Vast sums of money pour into the illicit economy, distorting normal economic functions and creating a climate of impunity where powerful criminal organizations operate with seemingly little fear of consequences. This isn't just about drug-related crimes; the pervasive influence of drug cartels spills over into other areas, increasing the occurrence of extortion, kidnapping, and other violent crimes. The consequences ripple through society, undermining the rule of law and eroding public trust in institutions.

Understanding the relationship between poverty and crime is crucial. High levels of socioeconomic inequality, a characteristic of many Latin American countries, create a breeding ground for crime. Lack of economic opportunities, limited access to education and healthcare, and inadequate housing all contribute to social unrest and desperation. Individuals and communities struggling under these conditions may resort to criminal activities as a means of survival or out of a sense of frustration and hopelessness. This isn't simply a matter of individual choices; it reflects systematic failures to address deep-rooted social and economic issues. Effective crime prevention strategies must therefore address the underlying causes of inequality.

Furthermore, the effectiveness of justice systems varies widely across Latin America. While some countries have made significant strides in modernizing their legal frameworks and strengthening their law enforcement capacities, others continue to struggle with corruption, a lack of resources, and bureaucratic inefficiencies. These shortcomings hinder effective prosecution, leading to high levels of impunity and perpetuating cycles of violence. The justice system itself, intended to protect citizens and uphold the law, can sometimes become part of the problem, either through direct involvement in criminal activity or through a failure to provide equal access to justice for all. Addressing this disparity requires comprehensive judicial reforms, focusing on increased transparency, accountability, and fair access to legal representation.

Cultural factors also play a significant role. Traditional practices and beliefs can influence attitudes towards crime and punishment. For instance, certain cultural norms may place a higher value on personal relationships than on strict adherence to formal laws. Moreover, the legacy of colonialism and its imposition of Western legal models without adequate consideration of local customs and traditions has created further complexities in understanding and addressing crime. An effective justice system must consider these cultural nuances and develop strategies that are both responsive to local realities and effective in upholding the rule of law. One-size-fits-all approaches rarely yield the desired results.

The challenge lies in forging a path towards sustainable solutions. It requires a multi-faceted approach, combining effective law enforcement, judicial reform, and social programs designed to address the root causes of crime and inequality. Strengthening community policing initiatives, improving access to education and job training, and promoting social inclusion are vital steps in creating safer and more just societies. Investing in preventative measures may seem less dramatic than reacting to crime but ultimately offers a more sustainable approach, breaking the cycles of violence and poverty. International cooperation is also essential, sharing best practices, providing technical assistance, and working collaboratively to dismantle transnational criminal organizations.

Addressing the issue of Latin American crime and justice isn't merely a matter of combating criminal activities. It's a complex undertaking that involves addressing deep-seated inequalities, reforming institutions, and fostering cultural understanding. It demands a holistic approach that acknowledges the historical context, the impact of the drug trade, the role of socioeconomic factors, and the importance of cultural sensitivity. Only by embracing a comprehensive and multi-faceted strategy can we hope to create a more just and equitable future for the people of Latin America. This involves a sustained commitment from governments, civil society, and international partners working together to foster lasting change. This requires not just reacting to symptoms, but addressing the underlying disease plaguing these societies.

5.1 Historical Context

The Spanish conquest of the Americas profoundly reshaped Latin American societies, leaving an indelible mark on their legal and criminal justice systems. Pre-Columbian societies, diverse in their structures and customs, possessed their own intricate systems of conflict resolution and social control, often intertwined with religious and spiritual beliefs. These varied greatly from the Inca Empire's centralized bureaucracy to the decentralized governance of numerous indigenous groups. The arrival of Europeans, however, initiated a brutal process of colonization, dismantling existing social orders and imposing foreign legal frameworks. The Spanish, fueled by the pursuit of wealth and power, implemented a system of law largely based on Roman and Canon law, adapted to suit the colonial context. This legal framework served primarily to consolidate Spanish control, exploiting indigenous populations and reinforcing a hierarchical social structure.

This imposed legal order often clashed with pre-existing indigenous customs and practices. Many indigenous legal traditions emphasized restorative justice, community reconciliation, and the resolution of disputes through mediation and negotiation. The Spanish system, in contrast, leaned towards retributive justice, emphasizing punishment and formal legal processes. This fundamental difference led to significant cultural misunderstandings and conflicts, exacerbating existing social inequalities. While Spanish law ostensibly provided a framework for order and governance, it frequently functioned as an instrument of oppression, further marginalizing and disenfranchising indigenous communities. The legacy of this colonial imposition continues to shape contemporary legal and criminal justice systems across the region.

The nineteenth and twentieth centuries witnessed significant political and social upheavals across Latin America, including independence movements, wars of liberation, and periods of authoritarian rule. These turbulent periods profoundly affected the development of legal frameworks. While many nations sought to establish independent legal systems, the influence of their colonial past remained a persistent factor, often manifesting in enduring social inequalities and institutional biases. The legacy of colonialism, coupled with internal conflicts and socio-economic disparities, has contributed to high crime rates and challenges in achieving effective criminal justice.

The rise of drug trafficking in the latter half of the 20th century added another layer of complexity to the already multifaceted landscape of crime and justice in Latin America. The involvement of powerful cartels and organized crime networks has overwhelmed many national justice systems, undermining the rule of law and fostering widespread corruption. Drug trafficking not only fuels violence and instability but also profoundly impacts legal institutions, often corrupting judges, police officers, and other key actors within the justice system. The scale of the problem often surpasses the capacity of state institutions to respond effectively. This has led to numerous attempts at reform, ranging from increased law enforcement to strategies focused on drug prevention and harm reduction.

Furthermore, the drug trade's economic implications are vast, creating vast wealth for criminal organizations and further exacerbating existing socio-economic inequalities. It has fueled conflict and violence in many regions, weakening the rule of law and creating a climate of impunity. Consequently, the region has experienced extremely high rates of homicides, kidnappings, and other violent crimes. The challenge now is to address the complex interplay between historical legacies, socio-economic disparities, and the drug trade in designing effective and equitable justice systems capable of protecting vulnerable populations. Understanding this historical context is crucial to analyzing and addressing the contemporary challenges facing Latin American nations in their quest for justice. The need for comprehensive strategies that tackle the root causes of crime, foster inclusive development, and strengthen institutions remains paramount. The path towards sustainable solutions requires confronting the ongoing legacies of the past while adapting to the unique realities of the present. Only through such a comprehensive approach can Latin America hope to build more just and equitable societies for all its citizens.

5.2 Drug Trade's Impact

The drug trade's relentless expansion across Latin America has fundamentally reshaped the region's social fabric, leaving an indelible mark on its legal systems and societal structures. Its pervasive influence extends far beyond the trafficking routes themselves; it corrupts governments, fuels violence, and undermines the rule of law, creating a climate of fear and instability that impacts every aspect of daily life. The sheer scale of the problem necessitates a multifaceted approach, one that transcends simple law enforcement strategies and addresses the underlying socioeconomic factors that contribute to its persistence.

Corruption, a seemingly unavoidable consequence of the drug trade's immense wealth, weakens state institutions from within. Law enforcement agencies, courts, and even political leaders can become compromised, hindering effective prosecution and facilitating the impunity enjoyed by powerful drug cartels. This pervasive corruption erodes public trust and discourages citizens from reporting crimes, further empowering criminal organizations and creating a vicious cycle of lawlessness. The very foundations of justice are threatened when those entrusted to uphold the law are instead complicit in its subversion.

Beyond corruption, the drug trade fuels an alarming escalation in violence. Rival cartels clash violently over territory and control, resulting in staggering murder rates and widespread insecurity. Communities living in areas affected by drug trafficking often become battlegrounds, caught between warring factions and lacking the protection of a functional state. This violence, often characterized by extreme brutality, leaves deep psychological scars on survivors, perpetuating a cycle of trauma that hinders social development and reconciliation.

The economic consequences are equally devastating. Drug-related activities often displace legitimate businesses, crippling local economies and leaving entire communities reliant on the drug trade for survival. This economic dependence creates a powerful incentive for continued participation in illicit activities, making it exceptionally difficult to break the cycle of drug-related crime. The consequences extend to legitimate businesses, deterred from investing in regions plagued by violence and uncertainty.

However, the impact of the drug trade extends far beyond immediate violence and economic disruption. It severely undermines the ability of states to provide basic services to their citizens. With resources diverted to combatting drug trafficking, essential services such as education, healthcare, and infrastructure development are often neglected, exacerbating existing social inequalities and further marginalizing vulnerable populations. This creates a fertile ground for recruitment into criminal organizations, offering a semblance of economic opportunity and social status that is otherwise absent.

Addressing the drug trade's profound impact requires a comprehensive and collaborative strategy. This demands strengthened law enforcement, coupled with effective judicial systems capable of prosecuting those involved in drug trafficking, while also emphasizing rehabilitation and social reintegration programs. Moreover, tackling the socioeconomic factors that drive participation in the drug trade is crucial. This necessitates investments in education, job creation, and community development initiatives that provide alternative sources of income and opportunity, particularly in areas most affected by drug trafficking. Furthermore, fostering international cooperation is essential, facilitating the sharing of intelligence, resources, and best practices in combating this global menace.

Ultimately, overcoming the drug trade's devastating effects requires a holistic approach that acknowledges its multi-faceted nature. Strengthening state institutions, addressing the root causes of participation, and promoting international cooperation are all indispensable components of a comprehensive strategy. Without tackling these interconnected issues, Latin America will continue to grapple with the devastating consequences of this transnational criminal enterprise, hampering its social, economic, and political development. The road to recovery is long and arduous, requiring sustained commitment, innovation, and unwavering determination at all levels of society and government. The fight against the drug trade is not simply a battle against criminal organizations, but a fight for the soul of the region.

6 Middle Eastern Legal Systems

The Middle East, a region of immense cultural and historical depth, presents a fascinating legal landscape. Its legal systems are not monolithic; instead, they represent a complex interplay between Islamic law, often referred to as Sharia, and various secular legal frameworks adopted by different nations. Understanding this dynamic requires appreciating the significant influence of religious principles on legal processes and outcomes while acknowledging the diverse secular legal systems operating concurrently. This interaction is not always harmonious; sometimes, it results in tensions and challenges in the administration of justice.

Islamic law, derived from the Quran and the Sunnah (prophetic traditions), forms a foundational element for many legal systems in the region. However, its application varies significantly across countries. Some states fully integrate Sharia into their legal codes, while others utilize it selectively, alongside secular laws borrowed from civil or common law traditions. The interpretation and implementation of Sharia also differ depending on the prevailing school of jurisprudence and the specific legal context. This leads to significant diversity in legal practices, even within the same broad religious framework.

Secular legal frameworks, inspired by Western legal models, are increasingly prominent across several Middle Eastern nations. These frameworks often address areas of law not explicitly covered by Sharia, such as commercial law or aspects of criminal procedure. The adoption of secular laws frequently reflects a conscious effort to modernize legal systems and align them with international standards, particularly in areas such as human rights and criminal justice reform. This process of legal modernization is, however, often complex and fraught with political and social challenges.

Navigating the legal landscape of the Middle East requires an understanding of how these religious and secular elements interact in practice. For example, family law often incorporates elements of Sharia, concerning issues like marriage, divorce, inheritance, and child custody. In contrast, criminal law may incorporate secular principles related to evidence and due process. This blending of legal traditions presents both opportunities and challenges. While it allows for legal systems that reflect both cultural values and contemporary legal principles, the tension between Sharia and secular law can also create uncertainty and inconsistency in legal outcomes. Interpretations often differ, making it crucial to carefully examine the specific legal context within each country. Cultural nuances further complicate the picture. Tribal customs and traditions, often deeply rooted in the social fabric, can significantly impact how legal matters are understood and resolved. Concepts of honor, shame, and family obligations may influence perceptions of criminality and the preferred means of dispute resolution. These cultural dynamics frequently interact with formal legal frameworks, shaping how laws are implemented and interpreted on the ground. For example, tribal mediation or reconciliation might play a significant role in resolving disputes before formal legal channels are engaged.

The administration of justice in the Middle East is therefore not simply a matter of applying codified laws. It involves a complex negotiation between religious principles, secular legal frameworks, and deeply ingrained cultural norms. This interplay creates a dynamic and constantly evolving legal system, requiring a nuanced understanding to comprehend its complexities and challenges. Ignoring these cultural aspects risks misinterpreting legal processes and outcomes. A thorough analysis of these interwoven legal threads is crucial for any comprehensive understanding of the Middle East's diverse legal landscape. Understanding the specific cultural context is as vital as understanding the legal text itself. Only then can a fair and accurate assessment of justice administration within the region be made.

6.1 Islamic Law's Influence

Islamic law, derived from the Quran and Sunnah (the Prophet Muhammad's teachings and practices), significantly shapes legal systems across many Middle Eastern and North African nations. Its influence extends far beyond criminal justice, impacting family law, commercial transactions, and personal conduct. Understanding its principles is crucial for comprehending the region's legal landscape. Unlike Western systems rooted in codified statutes or precedent, Islamic law embraces a complex interplay of scriptural interpretation, scholarly consensus, and juristic reasoning. This dynamism contributes to variations in its application across different countries and communities.

The core tenets of Islamic law prioritize justice, fairness, and the preservation of societal order. Crimes are often classified according to their severity, reflecting the harm inflicted on individuals and society. Punishments, often prescribed in the Quran or Sunnah, aim to deter criminal behavior, compensate victims, and promote societal rehabilitation. However, the application and interpretation of these punishments vary widely depending on the legal school (madhab) followed and prevailing social norms. Modern legal reforms in many Muslim-majority countries have attempted to reconcile traditional Islamic legal principles with the demands of modern nation-states.

For instance, the concept of hudud punishments, prescribed for specific offenses like theft or adultery, often elicits considerable debate. Some argue for their strict adherence based on scriptural mandates, while others advocate for alternative sentencing methods, citing concerns about human rights and proportionality. The interpretation and implementation of hudud highlight the ongoing tension between religious legal traditions and contemporary legal norms. This tension is further complicated by the presence of secular legal codes existing alongside Islamic law. Many Middle Eastern countries have dual legal systems, one based on Islamic principles and another adhering to secular laws, often dealing with separate aspects of life or specific populations.

The influence of Islamic law on criminal procedure is also considerable. Witness testimony holds significant weight, with specific requirements outlined for acceptable witnesses. The emphasis on evidence and due process aims to ensure fair trials, though challenges remain in ensuring equal access to justice and protecting the rights of all defendants. The role of religious courts in some jurisdictions complicates matters further, leading to varying levels of integration with the broader national legal system. The extent of this integration can be impacted by the degree of theocracy or the strength of the secular government.

Furthermore, Islamic law's impact extends beyond formal legal systems, influencing social attitudes towards crime and punishment. Religious norms and values shape perceptions of criminality, impacting reporting practices, victim support, and the broader social response to criminal acts. Community involvement in dispute resolution, reflecting traditional mediation practices, persists in many areas, offering an alternative avenue for conflict resolution alongside formal legal channels. However, modern challenges like increasing urbanization and globalization often test the adaptability of traditional mechanisms. The complexities of integrating ancient religious legal principles with the exigencies of a modern legal system—one constantly confronted by new offenses, technologies, and social conditions—remain a central concern for many Muslim-majority nations. It also presents a significant area of scholarly and legal debate. The intersection of religious law with modern needs shapes ongoing policy decisions, particularly regarding criminal justice. Balancing these competing forces will continue to drive legal and social change in the region for years to come. The study of these ongoing adaptations and their implications provides a window into the dynamics of a globalized world where legal and cultural traditions interact. These are not mutually exclusive; they are constantly shaping and reshaping one another. The result is a legal system that is both ancient and modern, rooted in religious tradition yet engaging with the challenges of the contemporary world. This ongoing adaptation underscores the dynamism and enduring relevance of Islamic law within the multifaceted legal frameworks of the Middle East.

6.2 Secular Legal Frameworks

Several Middle Eastern nations, while deeply rooted in Islamic legal traditions, have established robust secular legal frameworks. These frameworks, often influenced by European legal models, provide a system of laws separate from religious dictates, governing aspects of life such as contract law, property rights, and commercial transactions. This duality presents a fascinating case study in legal pluralism, where religious and secular laws coexist and, at times, intersect. The implementation and interpretation of these secular laws vary considerably across nations, reflecting diverse historical experiences and societal structures. Understanding these differences is key to comprehending the complexities of justice administration in the region.

The interaction between religious and secular laws isn't always harmonious. Conflicts can arise when secular laws challenge traditional norms or religious interpretations, leading to legal ambiguities and social tensions. For instance, issues related to personal status, such as marriage, divorce, and inheritance, often remain under the purview of religious courts, creating a potential disparity in legal treatment depending on religious affiliation. Navigating these overlapping legal domains requires careful consideration of both religious and secular legal precedents and their application in specific contexts. The impact of these interactions on social justice and equality is a crucial area of ongoing scholarly debate and policy discussion.

Consider, for example, the varying degrees of legal protection afforded to women under both secular and religious laws. While secular legal frameworks often aim for gender equality, the influence of traditional interpretations of religious texts can sometimes undermine these efforts. This creates a complex and often contradictory legal landscape, leading to differing legal outcomes for women depending on the specific legal forum and the interpretation applied. Addressing this requires not just legal reform but also a broader societal shift in attitudes and understanding. The need for transparent and accessible legal systems that ensure consistent application of secular law is paramount.

Furthermore, the development and application of secular legal frameworks in the Middle East have been significantly shaped by historical factors, including colonial legacies and the influence of international organizations. The adoption of codified legal systems, often based on European models, has been accompanied by both successes and challenges. While these systems aim to introduce principles of fairness and predictability, they often have to reconcile with pre-existing legal traditions and social norms. The process of adaptation and integration has been ongoing, and the success of secular legal frameworks depends significantly on the level of societal acceptance and support. Without this buy-in, even well-intentioned legal reforms may struggle to achieve their intended goals.

Ultimately, the efficacy of secular legal frameworks in the Middle East is intertwined with broader issues of governance, human rights, and social development. Strengthening institutions, promoting legal literacy, and ensuring equal access to justice are crucial steps in fostering a more just and equitable society. This requires not only a commitment to upholding the rule of law but also actively engaging with the complexities of cultural contexts and societal values. This holistic approach, encompassing legal reform, social dialogue, and institutional strengthening, is essential for ensuring that secular legal frameworks serve their intended purpose: to provide a just and fair system for all members of society, while recognizing and accommodating their diverse backgrounds and beliefs. The ongoing evolution of these systems presents a dynamic and rich area for further study and analysis. Only through careful observation and critical assessment can we fully appreciate the role of secular law in shaping the legal and social landscape of the Middle East.

6.3 Cultural Nuances in Justice

Understanding justice within a specific cultural context requires acknowledging deeply ingrained values and beliefs. For instance, honor-based violence, though condemned internationally, may be viewed differently within societies where the concept of family honor holds significant weight. Such cultural norms profoundly influence how crimes are perceived, reported, and ultimately, addressed within the legal system. This necessitates a nuanced approach, one that moves beyond simple categorizations of "right" and "wrong" to consider the complex interplay of cultural norms and legal frameworks.

The concept of shame and its role in shaping societal responses to wrongdoing is another crucial factor. In some cultures, the shame associated with a crime, particularly those impacting family reputation, might be seen as a sufficient punishment, even outweighing formal legal consequences. This can result in a preference for restorative justice practices that emphasize reconciliation and rehabilitation over strict punitive measures, a stark contrast to Western systems often focused on retribution. Understanding this fundamental difference in approach is vital for effective cross-cultural legal engagement.

Consider the varying perceptions of the state's role in dispensing justice. In certain societies, the state might be viewed as a distant, potentially untrustworthy entity, leading individuals to rely more on traditional mechanisms of conflict resolution, such as community elders or tribal councils. This reliance on non-state actors significantly impacts the effectiveness and reach of formal legal procedures. Conversely, in other societies, the state's authority is paramount, and deviations from its decrees are met with severe penalties. This contrasting view of the state's authority directly affects the application and implementation of laws.

Furthermore, the definition of evidence itself can vary significantly. What constitutes acceptable proof within one legal system might be inadmissible or considered weak evidence in another. The acceptance of oral testimony versus written documentation, the weight given to eyewitness accounts compared to forensic evidence - these disparities can significantly impact the outcome of legal cases. Consequently, legal professionals involved in cross-cultural contexts must be acutely aware of these differing evidentiary standards.

Legal processes, often assumed to be universally equitable, can be influenced by cultural biases. These biases might manifest in different ways, from the selection of jurors to the interpretation of legal texts. Implicit biases, ingrained cultural perspectives and stereotypes, can affect judgments unconsciously, leading to disparities in the treatment of defendants based on their cultural background or social standing. Recognizing and addressing these biases is critical to ensuring fairness within the legal process and promoting impartial justice.

The impact of colonialism on legal systems in formerly colonized regions continues to shape contemporary perceptions of justice. Inherited legal frameworks, often ill-suited to local contexts, may clash with deeply rooted cultural values and traditional dispute resolution mechanisms. This can lead to a lack of trust in the formal legal system and a preference for informal methods that are more in line with cultural norms. Effectively addressing this conflict necessitates a careful consideration of history and its lingering influences on contemporary legal practice.

Finally, international cooperation in criminal justice requires bridging significant cultural gaps. Extraditing a suspect, for example, might seem straightforward in principle, yet the process is often complicated by differences in legal procedures, evidentiary standards, and cultural considerations regarding human rights. A failure to acknowledge and navigate these cultural nuances can result in ineffective and unjust outcomes. Effective cross-cultural justice requires a commitment to understanding and respecting these differences, fostering collaboration, and promoting dialogue to create truly equitable and efficient global justice systems. The pursuit of justice, therefore, needs to be understood not just as a legal pursuit, but as a cultural one, necessitating empathy, respect, and a dedication to bridging deep-seated cultural divides.

7 Conclusion: Towards a Global Dialogue

The preceding chapters have meticulously documented the vast and multifaceted landscape of global crime and justice. From the intricacies of common and civil law systems in the West to the deeply rooted cultural influences shaping approaches in Asia, Africa, Latin America, and the Middle East, a clear picture emerges: there's no single, universally applicable model for addressing criminality. Understanding this diversity is not merely an academic exercise; it's fundamental to building truly effective and equitable global justice systems.

The persistent challenges posed by transnational crime, such as drug trafficking and cybercrime, demand international cooperation on an unprecedented scale. These crimes often transcend national borders, requiring collaborative efforts to investigate, prosecute, and prevent them. Effective collaboration necessitates mutual understanding and respect for differing legal traditions and cultural perspectives. We cannot effectively combat global crime while simultaneously ignoring the diverse ways different societies conceptualize justice.

A crucial aspect of fostering this cooperation lies in promoting cross-cultural legal education and exchange programs. These programs can facilitate dialogue between legal professionals from different jurisdictions, fostering mutual understanding of each other's systems and approaches. This shared knowledge can pave the way for more effective collaborations, allowing for the development of joint strategies to address transnational criminal activity. Such initiatives are not merely beneficial; they are essential for global security and justice.

Furthermore, the exchange of best practices between different justice systems can significantly improve the effectiveness of global crime-fighting efforts. For example, the restorative justice models prevalent in many Asian societies could offer valuable insights for Western systems grappling with high recidivism rates. Similarly, the community-based approaches to justice found in some African societies could provide inspiration for strengthening local law enforcement and crime prevention initiatives worldwide. Learning from each other is paramount.

However, simply transferring models from one context to another is unlikely to yield optimal results. The effectiveness of any justice system is profoundly shaped by its socio-cultural context. Therefore, any attempt at cross-cultural exchange must prioritize adaptation and contextualization. A successful approach will involve a deep understanding of the specific social, economic, and political dynamics of each setting. Blindly transplanting legal models ignores the critical role of context.

Looking ahead, a more nuanced understanding of the interplay between culture, law, and crime is crucial. This requires continued interdisciplinary research that draws upon the insights of sociology, anthropology, political science, and criminology, among other fields. We need sophisticated research methods, including comparative case studies and cross-national surveys, to gain a deeper understanding of these intricate relationships. Such thorough research is the bedrock of informed policy-making.

This comprehensive analysis underscores the limitations of adopting a single, universal approach to global crime. The diverse legal traditions and cultural perceptions explored throughout this book highlight the complexities inherent in defining and addressing criminality on a global scale. Recognizing this diversity is not a matter of relativism but a necessary precondition for creating more just and effective global justice systems.

The path forward involves a sustained commitment to cross-cultural dialogue, collaboration, and the exchange of best practices. This requires not only the cooperation of legal professionals but also the active engagement of policymakers, civil society organizations, and international bodies. Building trust and mutual understanding is essential for fostering collaborative efforts to tackle transnational crime. It is a long-term commitment.

Ultimately, the goal is to create a more equitable and effective system of global justice. This means ensuring that all societies have access to fair and impartial justice systems, regardless of their cultural or economic circumstances. This requires a concerted effort to address inequalities and injustices at both the national and international levels. Only through genuine commitment to equity can true progress be made.

This journey necessitates ongoing research to refine our understanding of the complex interplay between culture, law, and crime. It demands continuous dialogue to bridge cultural divides and facilitate the sharing of best practices. Above all, it calls for a sustained commitment to fostering a truly global understanding of justice—a justice that embraces diversity while upholding fundamental principles of fairness and equity for all. The task ahead is ambitious, but the pursuit of a more just and equitable world necessitates nothing less. The future of global justice hinges on our collective ability to engage in meaningful cross-cultural dialogue and collaborative action. The journey toward a more just and equitable world demands our continued dedication. The pursuit of global justice is an ongoing process, and future generations will continue to refine and improve our understanding and response to these complex global challenges.

7.1 Cross-Cultural Understanding

Understanding diverse cultural perspectives on criminality is paramount. Consider the stark differences in how theft is viewed: in some cultures, it's a deeply shameful act that severely impacts family honor, demanding significant community-based restorative measures. In others, it may be viewed more pragmatically, focusing on restitution and punishment through the formal legal system. This fundamental difference illustrates the complexities inherent in a globalized world grappling with cross-border crime. We must move beyond simple comparisons and start understanding the intricate web of social, economic, and historical factors that shape perceptions of crime.

Effective cross-cultural communication necessitates more than just linguistic fluency; it demands genuine empathy and a willingness to engage with unfamiliar perspectives. Active listening, seeking clarification, and being open to alternative interpretations are vital skills. Developing this skill set empowers professionals to navigate cross-cultural interactions with greater sensitivity and avoid misinterpretations that can hinder justice. This involves acknowledging one's own cultural biases and actively working to mitigate their impact. For example, a judge from a common law system might unintentionally impose Western notions of fairness on a defendant from a community where restorative justice is the norm.

The role of cultural intermediaries in resolving cross-cultural conflicts cannot be overstated. These individuals, deeply rooted in both cultures involved, bridge the communication gap, facilitating understanding and negotiation. They possess invaluable knowledge of cultural norms, practices, and sensitivities, enabling them to translate not just words, but also underlying meanings and intentions. Utilizing their expertise helps ensure that all parties feel heard and respected, improving the odds of achieving fair and equitable outcomes in legal and other dispute resolution processes. The involvement of such experts is crucial for fostering mutual trust and avoiding misunderstandings that could escalate conflicts.

Furthermore, understanding the history of a region is essential for comprehending its current approach to justice. Colonial legacies, for instance, have profoundly shaped legal systems in many parts of the world, leaving behind lasting impacts on attitudes towards authority, law enforcement, and the role of the individual within society. Ignoring these historical contexts risks misinterpreting contemporary practices and undermines effective engagement. A deeper understanding of historical power dynamics and their implications on the current legal landscape allows for a more nuanced and accurate analysis of cultural responses to crime.

Effective cross-cultural communication is not a one-size-fits-all approach; it requires flexibility and adaptability. The methods that work in one context may prove entirely inappropriate in another. Professionals engaging with diverse populations need to recognize this and develop a flexible toolkit of approaches, adapting their strategies as needed to effectively communicate with individuals from different backgrounds. This continuous learning process, fueled by ongoing research and self-reflection, allows for greater effectiveness and avoids the risk of imposing one's own cultural norms. Respect for diversity is the core of this flexible approach to communication.

Building bridges across cultures requires sustained effort and commitment. It demands patience, respect, and a genuine interest in understanding different perspectives. This proactive engagement fosters trust and facilitates cooperation, which is essential for addressing the complex challenges posed by cross-border crime and fostering a more just and equitable global system. Continuous learning, reflection, and open communication are not just beneficial but absolutely necessary for building strong, reliable bridges of understanding in this increasingly interconnected world. Only through collaborative efforts and mutual respect can effective and fair solutions be found.

Ultimately, effective cross-cultural understanding is not merely a theoretical concept but a practical necessity. It is vital for professionals who work in fields affected by cross-cultural interactions, from law enforcement and the judiciary to social work and international relations. Embracing this understanding allows for more effective communication, fairer legal processes, and the development of solutions tailored to the specific cultural contexts in which crime occurs. Without it, efforts to combat crime will remain fragmented and ultimately less effective. The success of our global response to crime depends on this crucial element of cross-cultural competence.

7.2 Future Directions in Justice

The future of justice hinges on embracing a truly global perspective, moving beyond simplistic comparisons and towards nuanced understanding. We must recognize that "justice" itself is a culturally constructed concept, its meaning shaped by historical experiences, social structures, and deeply held values. Therefore, future efforts must prioritize collaborative research initiatives, bringing together legal scholars, anthropologists, sociologists, and community leaders from diverse backgrounds. These cross-disciplinary teams can analyze the effectiveness of various justice models, not to declare one superior, but to identify best practices adaptable to different contexts.

International cooperation is no longer a luxury, but a necessity. Sharing information on successful crime prevention strategies, innovative restorative justice programs, and effective methods for addressing transnational crime is crucial. This involves fostering open dialogue between nations, facilitating the exchange of legal professionals and expertise, and supporting the development of international legal frameworks that respect cultural diversity while upholding fundamental human rights. This isn't about imposing a single model of justice, but about creating a shared understanding of common goals and finding pathways to achieve them.

Technology presents both challenges and opportunities. Data analytics can help identify crime trends, predict potential outbreaks of violence, and improve resource allocation. However, ethical considerations are paramount. We must ensure data privacy, prevent biases in algorithmic decision-making, and protect vulnerable populations from surveillance overreach. Responsible technology integration requires careful planning, robust oversight, and ongoing public dialogue to mitigate risks and maximize benefits. Technological advancements shouldn't lead to increased inequities or erosion of human rights.

Rethinking incarceration is another crucial area. The high rates of imprisonment in many countries, particularly in the West, have proven ineffective in reducing crime and often exacerbate social inequalities. Exploring alternative sentencing options, such as community-based restorative justice programs, mental health treatment, and vocational training, is essential. These alternatives can not only reduce prison populations, but also address the underlying causes of crime, creating safer and more equitable communities. This requires a shift from solely punitive measures towards approaches focused on rehabilitation and reintegration.

Addressing systemic biases in justice systems is paramount. Racial profiling, gender bias, and socioeconomic disparities continue to undermine the fairness and impartiality of legal processes worldwide. We need robust mechanisms for monitoring and addressing bias, including training for law enforcement and judicial personnel, data-driven analysis of disparities, and independent oversight bodies. Promoting diversity within justice institutions is also vital, ensuring that the system reflects the communities it serves and that diverse perspectives are incorporated into decision-making. True justice demands a commitment to fairness and equity for all.

Finally, educating future generations about global justice issues is imperative. Integrating comparative legal studies into school curricula, fostering cross-cultural understanding through educational exchanges, and promoting critical thinking about justice systems are vital steps. We must cultivate a generation that is not only knowledgeable about the different approaches to justice across the globe, but also capable of engaging in constructive dialogue and working towards a more just and equitable future. This includes promoting media literacy to counter misinformation and stereotypes related to crime and justice. A well-informed populace is better equipped to demand accountability and contribute to meaningful reform. Only through such collaborative, global efforts can we genuinely progress towards a future where justice is truly served for all.

www.ingramcontent.com/pod-product-compliance
Lightning Source LLC
LaVergne TN
LVHW022028200926
848481LV00007B/2582
* 9 7 9 8 3 4 8 5 9 6 0 9 5 *